IN MY MIND

A FAITH JOURNEY
THROUGH ROUGH SEAS

IN MY MIND

A FAITH JOURNEY
THROUGH ROUGH SEAS

PAUL G. TREMEWAN

Printed in the United States of America
ISBN 978-1-942285-10-6

Cover photo by Simon Jennings, Adobe Stock.com

Georgia Mountain Publishing, LLC
Suches, Georgia
www.georgiamountainpublishing.com

Acknowledgments

Thank you to all of the doctors, nurses, health care professionals, family and friends who were so supportive during Paul's illness. Your care and kindness made all the difference. I will be eternally grateful! God bless you!

Extra heartfelt gratitude goes out to the many special people whose love carried us through very rough seas:

ALS of Michigan (Southfield, MI) – Lisa Bardach

Church of the Holy Family (Grand Blanc, MI) – Colleen Argus, Angela Benchley, Linda Blondin, Jen Bolt, Martha Bonifazi, Carole Cocagne, Barb Daily, Leena DuPris, Theresa Dyer, Laura Fulco, Barb Gleason, Brian Holyfield, Vicky Holyfield, Laura Johnson, Amy Macksood, Paula Moors, Vanessa Pacheco, Sharon Peasel, Paula Rainey, Nancy Rapuyan, RCIA Class, Ellen Robbins, Carla Sharp, Pat Spoelhof, Sheila Starks, Mary Sterling, Meg Vaughn, Ellen Venus, Linda Waggoner, Janet Waters, Maddie White, Heather Williams, Cindi Wygoskey

Civil War Reenactors – North and South who served with Paul

Doctors – Dr. Gary King (Linden, MI), Dr. Arnold Markowitz (Keego Harbor, MI), Dr. Martin Ulrich (Grand Blanc, MI)

Family – Mary Kaye Burke, Pam Crawford, Allan Freeman, Emily Freeman, Georgerobert Freeman, Jeraldine Freeman, Jerome Freeman, Kevin Freeman, Ronald Freeman, Sue Henderson, Vicki Jones, Wayne Jones, Ruben Meza, Patti Nicholson, Ross Nicholson, David Pobocik, Mark Pobocik, Michael Pobocik, Tracie Pobocik, Allison Spaniola, Emily Tremewan, Jennifer Tremewan, Joanna Tremewan, Katlin Tremewan, Rob Tremewan, Samantha Tremewan, Terry Tremewan, Cheryl Wason, Tom Wason, Bill Welch, Carol Welch

Friends – Judy Allen, Karolyn Baker, Ken Baker, Barb Banks, Chris Berent, Janis Brooker, Robin Brooker, Dick Brown, Ruth Brown, Dave Chase, Kathleen Clarke, Maureen Corser, Jackie Culnon, Judy Dawson, Roger Duncan, Glory Elzy, Nora Fisher, Denny Gazso, Sue Goering, Steve Golder, Mike Greenfield, Betty Harris, Mary Jo Holstine, K.J. Hooten, Gary Hoppe, Judy Hoppe, Doug Imlach, Glenda Johnston, Kathy Maitland, Barry McGhan, Carylon Meeker, E. Tom Mims, D.M.D., Paula Morse, Steve Nikoloff, Hugh Orr, Alta Parsons, Nicole Pellegrino, Justine Phelps, Sally Pierson, Jim Rosser, Pat Rosser, Peg Russell, Sandy Stableford, Margaret Taylor, Len Thomas, Nancy Watson, Bruce Webb, Paul Victor Yengle

Grand Blanc Genesys Regional Medical Center (Grand Blanc, MI) – All the staff who cared for Paul

Grand Blanc Rehab (Grand Blanc, MI) – All the staff who cared for Paul

H-Care Health Care (Flint, MI) – Tunde Akindele, Bev Dempsey, Barb Hill, Raymond Hubble, Brooke Jordan, Dena Pratt, Toni Scandrick, Maxine Scott, Trisha Ware

Henry Ford Hospital (Detroit, MI) – Helen Foley, Dr. Daniel Newman, Stephanie Ryczko

Holy Redeemer Roman Catholic Church (Burton, MI) – Cindy Anderson, Fr. Steve Anderson, Emily Arthur, Margaret Carter, Amber Jones, Ed Munger, Kathy Patterson, Jaymie Petronzi, RCIA class, Dan Schmit, Vickie Sturgess

Home Helpers (Grand Blanc, MI) – Martina Ortiz, Mike Ortiz, David Pobocik, Eliza Wong

North Carolina Neighbors – Ally Davis, Bill Fargo, Judy Fargo, Peter Goundrey, Suda Goundrey, Bill Lewis, Kevin Mohan, Sheila Mohan

St. Clare's Episcopal Church (Blairsville, GA) – Estelle Alexander, Ken Alexander, Kay Cahoon, Leslie Davis, B. J. Foster, Evie Greene, Nancy Hopkins, Judie Kean, Fr. Thomas Martin, Bob Montgomery, Delores Montgomery, Amy Pollin, Edie Pollin, Judy Rich, Carol Sayer, Jonathan Sayer, Fran Smith, Jim Smith, Camille Troth, Dr. Mary Beth Wiles, Fr. Frank Wilson, Suzanne Harris Wilson, Eloise Wolfersteig

And a special thank you to Barbara Harkins of Georgia Mountain Publishing for her assistance in getting this book ready for publication.

Much love!
Gloria Tibbetts

Contents

(continued)

The Stories

2 Corinthians 4:16

So we do not lose heart.
Though our outer self is wasting away,
our inner self is being renewed day by day.

Prologue

On December 11, 2013, I lost my dad, Paul George Tremewan, to a horrible degenerative disease, ALS. It is striking how truly unfair life can be. Losing a loved one for any reason is hard, but losing my dad to ALS and bearing witness to his physical decline when he was still of sound mind was especially difficult for me and for everyone who knew and loved him.

What was remarkable was the positive outlook on life and sense of humor he himself maintained to the very end despite his situation. Moreover, the impact he had on so many people up to the end of his own life was unique. Even near the end, when he had no use of his arms and legs, no ability to speak, he still had a certain magnetism that drew people to him. Nurses who cared for him and who knew him for only a brief period of time came to his memorial service. One nurse came to the hospital on the last day of his life on this earth to say goodbye. He came bearing a six-pack of Guinness (my dad's favorite beer) and left in tears.

Dad was born on September 9, 1941 in the city of Flint, Michigan, Vehicle City and birthplace of General Motors. Despite spending a year in bed due to a serious illness as a child, he lived an active, healthy life up until the time he was diagnosed with ALS. Even after his diagnosis, he remained active until his body no longer accommodated his ambitions.

Dad grew up enjoying outdoor adventures, camping, hunting and fishing in what many refer to as "God's country" in beautiful northern Michigan. He graduated from Flint Central High School, class of 1959, where he was a much-loved Flint Central Indian mascot for four years. After high school he attended junior college, where he worked in the planetarium and met my mom. From there he went on to graduate from the

University of Michigan, followed by graduate studies at Eastern Michigan University and Wayne State University.

Ultimately, Dad made his career and his mark on the world as a teacher. He loved working with and lifting up underprivileged children. He specialized in teaching children to read, teaching history and most of all making it fun and interesting to learn. My dad was an avid, lifelong learner, a voracious reader and writer. He was a student and reenactor of the Civil War. He also authored a book on the Civil War entitled *As Near Hell As I Ever Expect To Be.* As a reenactor, he even had the opportunity (along with thousands of other reenactors) to play an extra in the movie *Gettysburg.* In the movie he was one of the thousands of casualties in Major General George Pickett's famous ill-fated charge on the Yankee center.

A transplant in the South (and to Confederate reenacting), after raising two kids, retiring and sailing together with my mom down to Florida to live for several years, Dad finally got his lifelong wish to move to a cabin in the woods when he and my mother relocated to the wooded hills of beautiful Murphy, North Carolina. My mom was suffering from terminal cancer, and so Dad cared for her at home until she passed. He immersed himself in Civil War studies and carpentry to divert his mind from sorrow to positive activities, unknowing at that time that he himself was afflicted with a terminal illness.

Dad loved to build all sorts of things, including boxes, bird houses, trunks, tables, etc. Even while living alone in his beloved cabin in the woods, he built himself a giant dining table just so he could host Thanksgiving dinner at his house for family and the wonderful, supportive friends he made at St. Clare's Episcopal Church in Blairsville, Georgia. That table always reminded me of the Last Supper table of Jesus.

One day, when talking to Dad on the phone, I noticed that he was slurring his words. I assumed that he had downed a few too many Guinesses, but this was not the case. He had recently been injured in an ATV accident while visiting Michigan, so when it became even more obvious that something was wrong, we thought that perhaps his collision with the tree had caused some neurological damage. After numerous tests, doctors concluded that Dad actually had rapid-onset ALS.

Around this time an angel came into his life. He fell in love again, and the two of them committed themselves to each other despite the dim prospects for the remainder of his life. My dad was giddy and happy and very much in love. But not long after, bliss gave way to a daily struggle for life. Anxiety, fear, pain, discomfort, loss of body function, loss of independence and the numerous indignities that accompany this evil disease incrementally took their toll. Nevertheless, he endeavored to survive. He persevered in the face of the tireless onslaught of ALS, perhaps well past the point others would have thrown in the towel and said, "Enough is enough." He wanted to live. He dreamed. He loved and was loved back. He inspired. He had so many friends, family, former students, former classmates, colleagues and Civil War reenacting buddies to reach out to, so much to live for, so much left to do, but precious little time. He fought the disease. He hoped and prayed, but no miracle or cure was forthcoming.

My dad progressed from slurred speech to inability to speak at all, to inability to swallow, which necessitated the installation of a feeding tube directly into his stomach. During this period Dad could still get around but was starting to lose control of his hands and the ability to hold up his head without a neck brace. Carpentry was no longer a feasible diversion. Dad said that he could identify with the Simon and Garfunkel song, "Slip Slidin' Away."

While his body was failing, his mind was still quite sharp, and now with his mortality dominating his thoughts, he wrote poems and little stories. The poems were written to capture his thoughts, his emotions and prayers. He wrote stories to capture and share funny and poignant experiences for posterity. He wrote until he could write no more.

Dad lost the ability to breathe through his mouth, and he had to have a tube installed in his trachea. He could no longer breathe overnight without the aid of a respirator and for only short periods of time during the day. My brilliant dad had become a prisoner in his own body. Amazingly, despite his severely degraded and unenviable quality of life, he maintained his famous sense of humor to the bitter end.

By November 2013, our conversations were reduced to him pointing his toe to letters of the alphabet on a board at the foot of his bed, but he still maintained his well-known sense of humor. During one of my last visits with him, although he was not long for this world, bedridden and with a grin on his face, he told me that he was going to get started working on his "bucket list." And did we ever have a great laugh about that one. Now Dad is gone, and I miss him.

Although he is no longer with us, he no longer suffers; and all who knew him are blessed with the fond memories of having known him. My dad, being the loving, caring soul he was, would have been quite thrilled and honored to have his writings published so as to give comfort or inspiration to those who may need it. It is my hope that this book can help anyone suffering from terminal illness find peace, and even if in but a small way help in the fight against ALS. This book is dedicated to the memory of my dad, Paul George Tremewan, and to those in spiritual need into whose hands this book may find its way. May they be at peace.

Rob Tremewan

The Poems

My Morning Prayer

My Heavenly Father, I thank you for the gift of another day,
    another chance to begin again.
I do not know what this day will bring, but I pray you will be
    with me to face whatever comes.
If I am to stand up, help me to stand bravely.
If I am to sit still, help me to sit quietly.
If I am to lie down, help me to lie patiently.
If I am to do nothing, help me do it reverently.
If I am to be a guinea pig in a research study, help me to teach
    the doctors what they need to know to cure ALS.
If I am to be cured, help me receive your power and gracefully
    and gratefully accept whatever healing is your will for me.
If I am to assist someone, help me to meet their needs.
If I am to die, help me to die peacefully and send your angels
    to bring me to your eternal presence.
I pray you will grant me your grace to make these words
    more than words.
I pray through your Son, Jesus Christ, son of Mary,
    my advocate and redeemer.
                    Amen.

(Adapted and integrated from many prayers.)

[September 2011]

Yesterday, Today and Tomorrow

O Lord. My God,
Father of Jesus Christ,
My Redeemer and my shepherd,
Give ear to my meditations.
Yesterday is gone,
Like a vapor, a dream,
Existing only as a fading memory
In the deep corners of our minds.
The future is an illusion,
Unfathomable, unknown,
A course beyond our human understanding
To forecast its components.
Despite our feeble attempts to know.

What we do have is the present.
As God's children we have today.
Our shepherd leads us through
The confusing maze of life's challenges.
He knows our names,
Our strengths and our weaknesses.
We do not know the path we are on,
But the shepherd does.

This today might be our last,
So we should live it as if it were.
Though plagued by fear,
Uncertainty, disease, pain,
Our own sins, foolishness,
Errors, or stupidity,
Today is the best day we have.

We must try to hold in abeyance
Our human weaknesses,
And rely on the grace and love of God
To get us through today.
Our confidence will wane.
We will fall down.
Our free will causes us to make mistakes.
But unless this is our last day,
We must get up and carry on,
And not give in to the quagmire
Of self-pity, fear and desperation.

Our solution lies in our faith
In God,
In our trust and confidence
In the promise
Jesus made to us,
He that believes in Me,
Shall not die,
But have life everlasting.
I believe . . .

[April 2011]

The Monster: ALS

I am being stalked by a monster . . .
I am his prey.
He wishes to destroy me.
Every day he looses thousands of microscopic arrows at me.
He aims at my synapses, destroying them one at a time.
His onslaught is relentless.
I am defenseless.
I face the biggest challenge of my life.

Slowly but surely, as my synapses die, others assume the burden,
    until they too are struck by his arrows.
Inexorably the voluntary body slows down, becomes
    overwhelmed, and shuts down.
All movement . . . speaking . . . swallowing . . . breathing . . .
    become memories.

To protect myself, I need armor.
An armor so specialized that the molecule-size arrows of the
    monster have no effect.
The armor, a brain-produced protein, used to be there.
It is gone now, out of production.
No one understands why.
Without it, the synapses are destroyed, one after the other.

Like a knight in shining armor, mounted on a magnificent steed,
  help is on the way.
An old acquaintance, ceftriaxone, emerges from the laboratories
  of the past.
As new armor, the protein reappears to destroy the arrows
  of the monster.
It slows down the attack, ends the onslaught.

The damage done cannot be repaired.
But a new plateau of being is possible.
No one knows how the body will compensate for the wounds
  received, the losses sustained.

But I am not in this battle alone, am I?
I think I'll stick around to see . . .

[October 2011]

In My Mind

In my mind . . .
In my mind I am ageless:
    Stuck somewhere between 7 and 70,
    Not old, not young,
    Retaining all the knowledge and wisdom of a lifetime.

In my mind . . .
In my mind I can do anything I have ever done:
    Run a mile in half an hour
    Climb a cliff
    Swim laps of an Olympic pool and not get tired
    Ride a bike up and down a mountain road
    Climb to the top of a 54-foot mast
    Drive 10 or 12 hours at a time
    Lift a bag of cement to my shoulder in one swift movement
    Chop down a tree
    Build a table
    Write a book, a poem, a love letter, a prayer.

In my mind . . .
In my mind I can be anywhere I have ever been:
    Canada, Mexico, England, France, Germany, Spain,
        Switzerland, New Zealand, Fiji
    Every state but one, Alaska
    In every house I ever called home
    In every bed I slept
    In every classroom I ever taught.

In my mind . . .
In my mind I can see everything I have ever seen:
    The Snowy Owl in winter
    The mountain lion in the canyon of the Ocoee
    The red sunset behind Longs Peak, Colorado
    Black snow
    The elk with rocking-chair antlers wandering
        through my campsite
    The grizzly bear watching me fish for trout
    The field of orange pumpkins in October
    The full moon behind the Empire State Building
    The Eiffel Tower
    The Tower of London
    Henry the VIII's codpiece
    The Rock of Gibraltar
    Hadrian's Wall
    Red-headed girls in Edinburgh
    Hundreds of ancient churches and cathedrals
    The smiling faces of loved ones I have lost along the way
    The total blackness 10 miles offshore in the Atlantic
    Penguins waddling ashore
    The pride in a student learning to read.

[continued]

In my mind . . .
In my mind I can smell everything I have ever smelled:
    The coal-burning furnace of my childhood
    The smoke of forest fires burning out of control
    The stench of dead fish on the beach of Acapulco
    The sulphurous vapors of Yellowstone
    Coffee, fresh-baked bread and bacon on Saturday mornings
    My children's diapers
    Salty air along the eastern seaboard
    Cow manure being shoveled out of the barn
    The fish markets in New York, Portland and Savannah.

In my mind . . .
In my mind I can hear everything I ever heard:
    My father's scream-like swearing
    My brother's cries from beatings
    My grandmother praying in Dutch
    My mother's child-like voice
    My coach's consternation at my snail-like pace
    The reaction when I scored a basket for the other team
    The thud when I dropped a girl I was trying to dip
    The doctor saying, "It's a boy!"
    My son's first cry, laugh, word
    The first time I ever said "I love you"
    The last breath of a dying wife
    The roar in the stadium when I did a war dance
        at football games
    The sweetness of grandchildren calling me "Gwanpodder"
    The thunder of Niagara Falls
    The jet-like sound of Old Faithful
    The rattles of a 6.2 earthquake
    The first time she said "I love you."

In my mind . . .
In my mind I can feel everything I ever felt:
    My first kiss
    My first heartbreak
    My first spanking
    My worst black eye
    My fractured skull
    The first time I made love
    The last time I made love
    The warmth of friendship
    The coldness of rejection
    The joy of loving and being loved
    The helplessness of caring for a loved one while she dies
    The shame of breaking other people's hearts.

In my mind . . .
In my mind I know:
    I have been blessed beyond all merit
    Loved beyond all expectations
    I am a child of God
    He is the anchor in my life
    I will not live forever
    I have ALS
    I must live with this disease, hoping and praying for the best,
        while preparing for the worst.
    I am not alone!

[October 2011]

15

The Flock

The sheep-like clouds are slowly grazing their way
    across the azure sky.
They make not a sound as the flock moves relentlessly west.
They leave the sky empty as the sun sets.
This flock will never come again.
Perhaps a new one will appear tomorrow to be shepherded
    across the sky.
I see them here and now, and reverence their passing.

[October 2011]

A Touch

In the middle of the night
While I lay sleeping
Flat on my back with my uncovered arms at my side,
Someone touched my right hand.
It was firm but gentle
And warm.

When I opened my eyes
The sensory shadow of the touch remained,
But no one was there,
At least I saw no one.
This was not the first time I have been visited,
And I hope not the last.

I don't know who it was.
I don't know if it was the same visitor each time.
Sometimes I feel a presence on my bed,
Other times a simple touch.
Each time I awaken to an empty room,
I am alone.

I think I know why I don't see anyone.
As a human being, I see with my eyes.
As a Christian, I see with the eyes of my heart.
These two ways of seeing are quite different.
My eyes see the physical world.
The eyes of my heart see the spiritual world.
I hope the touch comes again.

Maybe I will see something this time . . .

[November 2011]

Fasciculations

Our voluntary muscles are in constant communication
with our brains, our mainframe computers,
in a constant state of readiness.
They await the call to action,
to walk, run, lift, stand, roll over,
to swallow,
to speak,
to move.

Then ALS comes along,
Amyotrophic Lateral Sclerosis.
Synapses begin to burn out.
That brain-produced protein-protection
is no longer present.

Once the synapse is fried,
the "be-ready" signals from the brain
cannot reach the muscle fibers,
but the "I'm ready" signals from muscle fibers continue,
but cannot reach the brain.

The muscle fibers fasciculate,
they twitch,
desperately trying to re-establish the electric dialogue
with the brain
they have always known.

The fasciculations are completely random,
wherever synapses burn out they occur,
fibers twitch.
No predictable pattern,
just a futile attempt to do what they have always done.

As more and more synapses die,
more and more fibers are affected.
From head to toe,
voluntary muscle fibers twitch,
waiting for that signal
which never comes
as they wither away to uselessness.

But in a dream,
I discovered something the neurologists do not know.
Those little twitches, those spasms
which flit here, there, everywhere,
I know what they really are!

They are tiny mice
trapped inside our bodies,
running helter-skelter all over,
trying to find a way out.
But they keep bumping into stuff
as they frantically run amok
looking for a way to escape.

Gradually they slow down,
run out of energy,
and hibernate.
No more bumps,
beating their little heads against our skin,
trying to get out.
They give up
and like our muscles
go to sleep and shrivel up.
That's what fasciculations really are.

[November 2011]

Our Crosses

Many people carry crosses.
We did not ask for them.
We did not volunteer.
We're not sure how we got them.

We carry them wherever we go,
Day or night, awake or asleep,
They are ours to bear
Until the day we surrender to them.

Jesus carried His cross.
He did not have a choice.
He knew it was His mission
Until He said, "It is finished."

There is another place
A mystery we will all solve.
We believe it is love, peace,
No pain, no fear, no end.

Here on earth
Our burdens are temporary.
They get us down, wear us out,
They scare us, make us cry.

One day we all will graduate.
We'll leave our crosses behind
And take leave of this vale of tears.
We will surrender them and move on.

It is a one-way trip
To that mysterious place,
But we take nothing with us,
Not even our crosses.

[December 2011]

An Epiphany, of Sorts

Recently I had an epiphany, an awakening.
It was a quiet one.
But with the force of a lightning bolt,
I finally realized
I have Amyotrophic Lateral Sclerosis,
Otherwise known as ALS or Lou Gehrig's Disease.

My symptoms began fifteen months ago,
My diagnosis seven.
But it really did not sink in
Until one day, sitting home alone,
The conceptual reality of an untreatable, debilitating,
Terminal disease hit me in the gut.

Fear and panic and hopelessness,
Traveling at the speed of light,
Rose up through my chest to my throat,
Choking me,
And flowed out of my eyes
While I gasped for air.

For sixty-nine years I had been fairly healthy:
Childhood diseases, bumps and bruises, colds,
The flu, pink eye, pneumonia, a fractured skull,
Some torn ligaments, a ripped rotator cuff,
Some bloody noses, a few broken ribs, some sprains,
A couple of black eyes, and a hemorrhoid or two.
That's it!

Now I have ALS, the rapid onset, Bulbar kind.
My speech is almost gone,
Swallowing is almost a thing of the past.
My left arm is half as strong as my right.
Fine motor skills in my left hand are evaporating.
I have muscle spasms in my left shoulder and
      in my upper arms.
My muscle mass is shrinking,
And I drool!

I am in the first battle of a war I cannot win.
No one knows how long the war will last.
The licks I'll take are known,
But their sequence and severity are not.
This personal civil war of mine could end quickly,
Or last more than ten years.

At this point, I am in pretty good shape.
My brain works as well as it ever did.
I can see whatever I look at.
I can hear in spite of tinnitus.
I can smell all the aromas life offers.
I love . . . and I am loved.

Here I am, now seventy years old
Trying to figure out what I will do with the rest of my life,
But that's no different than what I have always done:
Making lists, dreaming dreams, wishing on a star,
Blowing out candles, looking for possibilities,
And praying . . .
Waiting for that peace that passes all human understanding.

[January 2012]

A Faith Journey

A faith journey is like a long voyage, alone, in a sailboat.
You have an idea about your destination
But along the way you are buffeted by earthly obstacles:
Rain, wind, tides, storms, enormous waves, and all sorts
    of leviathans of the dark.
You are also hindered by the hidden obstacles of the mind:
Fear, panic, loneliness, ignorance and unbelief.

Although we all leave from different ports,
Our destination as Christians is the same,
That place where we will spend eternity
Bathed in the light of a loving God.

No two voyages are the same.
We don't all start out with the same equipment,
    background, or preparation
But at some point in our lives we board our fragile boats,
    haul up the anchor,
And set sail for the most important journey of our lives.

My sporadic journey began many years ago:
Birth, baptism, confirmation, oblation,
And recently my reception into the Holy Catholic Church.
Along the way, over seventy years, I encountered love, birth,
    death, joy, sorrow,
Loss, gain, failure, success, sin, forgiveness, and now disease.

But through it all, from port to port, I was never alone.
That voice speaking to the ear of my heart,
Once so small
Has grown to speak to the very core of my being.

Now, closer than ever to that final glorious destination,
I have dropped anchor in a safe harbor,
Surrounded by love,
Where I write entries into my ship's log, and pray.
I have plenty of oil for my lamp
And keep watch for the Master to come.

[January 2012]

Blessings

Praise God
From whom all blessings flow . . .

Life is like a snowball rolling down a snow-covered hill.
It gets bigger, it collects more snow the farther it rolls.
It does not ask for more,
It just happens.
The same is true of blessings.

At birth we humans are a tabula rasa,
A blank slate on which we write the story of our lives,
On which we collect stuff: experiences, knowledge
    and memories.
We are the authors of our own story.

The older we are, the more stuff we have collected
And stored in our brains.
Among the collected stuff are blessings.
We did not ask for them,
They just happened.

My first blessing was the gift of life,
That was more than seventy-one years ago,
More like a blink of my eye.
Blessings have flowed to me all my life:
Family, friends, teachers, neighbors,
Children, students,
Even strangers.
Too many blessings to count.

One blessing stands out.
It happened twice.
For some it never happens.
The blessing of love.
Two wonderful women fell in love with me,
And I fell in love with them.

My college sweetheart married me.
We raised two children.
We were a couple for almost forty-seven years,
Until cancer took her away.

An old colleague from work twenty years ago
Came into my life and
In spite of my diagnosis of ALS
Committed her life to me
For the rest of my life.

Some blessings are more like miracles . . .

[May 2012]

Condemned To a Prison: Life Without Parole

I am condemned to a prison,
A life sentence without parole.
I did nothing to deserve it.
I said nothing to deserve it.
I thought nothing to deserve it.
I am diagnosed with Bulbar ALS,
Amyotrophic Lateral Sclerosis.

I am not the first.
I am not the last.
I have joined a special fraternity,
We who, one synapse at a time,
Lose all voluntary muscle control.
We become locked up in our own bodies.

Slowly, inexorably, we lose our abilities
To swallow,
To talk,
To smile,
To move our arms and legs,
To walk,
To hold up our heads,
To breathe.

We can see.
We can hear.
We can smell.
We can think.
We can still love.

As we move deeper into our personal prisons,
We are frustrated,
We are angry,
We are sad,
We are afraid,
We are adrift in a sea of memories,
We are lost in an ocean of dreams deferred or lost forever.
Some of us give up all hope.

We will spend the residue of our lives
Locked in our own personal prisons.
There is no parole,
No time off for good behavior,
No pardon,
No cure.

Saint Paul, my namesake, was imprisoned,
Beaten and in chains,
He prayed and sang.
He praised God.
He thanked God.
He glorified God.
He worshiped God.

I believe in God, the Father Almighty,
Creator of all that is, seen and unseen,
And His son Jesus, my redeemer and advocate.

[continued]

I pray God will grant me
The grace, strength and courage
To praise,
To thank,
To glorify,
To worship Him,
While I am imprisoned.
That He will send His Holy Angels
To escort me to His presence,
To see His face,
And dwell in His house forever.
Amen.

[August 2012]

A Voyage

Lord, I am sailing into a stormy fog-bound sea.
I have no instruments to guide me.
I am weak and confused,
Not knowing which way to go.

But, Lord,
You are my pilot,
You are my beacon,
You are my anchor.

Although I cannot see the way ahead,
The eyes of my mind see only darkness,
The eyes of my heart, my soul, see your light.

I know you await me
on that not too distant shore.
But I have heavy seas to go through
Before I enter your safe harbor.

I pray for courage and strength,
for your holy angels to be with me
through tumult and terror
As I sail to you.

[October 2012]

31

Character

Terminal disease is a crappy way
to test your character.
You are in decline,
you are confused,
you mourn your past,
you don't know what is next.

So, what do you do?
You can cry all the time.
You can bitch and moan.
You can scream.
You can make the lives of those around you
a living hell.
You can curl up into a fetal ball
and die.

I don't like any of those options.
I'd rather love and be loved.
I'd rather enjoy my family and friends.
I'd rather tell some funny stories.
I'd rather laugh a lot.
I'd rather give and receive lots of hugs.
I'd rather have a good drink
(through my stomach tube)!

Nothing I can do will change the outcome.
We all die sometime,
some sooner, some later than most.
Actual dying does not bother me.
If anything, the preliminary stuff does,
but not so much I want to dwell on it.

This is the time to celebrate the life I've had,
to remember great times,
experiences, places and people.
I have been made richer by my friends,
mellowed by my family,
blessed by the people who love me.

I am God's child.
We all are.
We are created in God's image.
We are expected to do something good,
sooner, not later; often, not seldom.
Love is to be our mantra.
I pray I have done, and will do, His will.

[October 2012]

33

A Look in the Mirror

I looked in the mirror the other day
and almost didn't recognize
the bearded old man
who was looking at me.

I never spent much time in front of a mirror,
not since I was a teenager
slicking down my hair with Vaseline.
Not since I was learning how to raise one eyebrow
and to wiggle my ears.
Now that I wear a beard,
my mirror time is reduced to
the monthly trim.

That man I saw in the mirror
has deep furrows in his forehead.
His eyes have crow's feet,
and nearly epicanthic folds.
His shaved head shines as if waxed.
His beard looks like salt and pepper steel wool.
Above his dark, piercing eyes
are undisciplined eyebrows.

That man in the mirror
looks a lot like me,
same forehead, same nose.
He looks like a much older brother, a cousin,
like the old-time photographs of Tremewans,
grandfathers and uncles long deceased.
He does not smile well,
his facial muscles don't work like they used to.

I know he is me,
transformed from a child
into a seventy-one-year-old man
whose face reflects a lifetime,
a multitude of experiences,
that carved the clay of his countenance
into the image he can only see
when he looks into a mirror.

How do we see ourselves
before we really look in a mirror?
Would old friends recognize us?
Would we recognize them?
Would we recognize ourselves?
Are we young, old, or just there?

That man I saw in the mirror,
I know him.
He loves and is loved in return.
He laughs, cries, smiles, frowns.
He thinks, creates, hopes, fears,
and believes . . .
He is like an old leather-bound book,
resting on a shelf,
worn around the edges,
but still a good read.

[October 2012]

Rock, Paper, Scissors

In that child's game,
A rock breaks scissors,
Scissors cut paper,
And paper covers rock.
But yesterday I learned,
Concrete trumps them all.

If you ever have to fall
Pick your destination carefully:
If indoors, pick a plush carpet, a pillow, a mattress.
If outdoors, pick tall grass, a pile of leaves, or
If it is summer, a pool,
If it is winter, a snow drift.

Falling is not the hard part,
The stop is.
Gravity is indifferent to your plight.
Gravity just takes you down
So you can test that fundamental law of physics:
Two objects cannot occupy
The same space at the same time.

I was reminded of the law
When I lost my balance and fell headfirst,
Not onto plush carpet, a pillow, a mattress,
Tall grass, a pile of leaves, a pool or snow,
But a concrete porch step.

They say when you are drowning
Your whole life flashes through your mind.
When I fell
I found myself thinking
Oh, Shit!

The human body is a remarkable thing,
Flexible, resilient, repairable,
And now we are developing spare parts.
But in a contest with concrete,
Concrete will win every time.

We don't bounce all that well.
When we hit something
It is a thud, a crunch, or a clunk.
I clunked!
I have seven staples in my head to prove it!

[October 2012]

Life As an Hourglass

I see my life as an hourglass.
I almost feel the grains of sand falling,
Incessantly, one after one.
I know they fall for all of us,
Not just for me.
But we are not aware,
We can't hear them,
They fall so silently.

When accident or illness threatens our future,
Our newly sharpened senses become aware
Of so many things
We never sensed before,
Especially our mortality.

When all is well and happy,
When we are comfortable,
We blindly go from experience to experience,
Never thinking about our last days.
Yet we all should look at life
As a terminal illness,
None of us will get out alive.

Saint Benedict reminds us to remember every day
That we will die.
This is not a bad thing to do.
It should keep us in mind of the blessings
We receive every day,
The beauty of the creation around us,
And the opportunity we have with each new day
To be and to do better
Than we have ever done before.

Because of ALS,
Amyotrophic Lateral Sclerosis,
I am acutely aware of the sand falling
In my personal hourglass.
Each grain of sand represents a synapse
That cannot transmit messages
To the voluntary muscles
Which would allow them to do the will of the brain.

I am not angry about this development,
This new turn of events.
It is pointless to be angry at facts
You have absolutely no control over.
Because of these circumstances,
My sand is falling
More quickly than most.
It is part of living with ALS.

[continued]

I am acutely aware
Of constant fatigue,
The loss of speech,
The inability to swallow,
The atrophy of my left arm,
The continuing weakness of all voluntary muscles,
And the steady increase in difficulty of breathing.

Some days I grieve for the man I used to be,
For the capabilities I used to have,
And wonder what will happen next.
But all that is a waste of time,
My remaining time is far too important
For me to labor over
What was or is to be.

We humans live in what has been called the vale of tears.
It is all we have ever known.
We were born here,
We will die here.
But there is more,
A mystery beyond our comprehension,
A mystery only solved by faith.

Some day the sand will stop falling,
When that last grain falls.
We don't know when or where,
But when it falls,
Our eyes close,
Our hearts stop beating,
And we take our last journey.

We are changed forever,
In an instant we awaken to a new life,
In a new place.
No one can tell us what it is like,
We can only believe the promise of old,
That those who believe
Shall not perish,
But have life everlasting.

Belief is not always easy.
The stresses and strains of life,
The temptations that surround us,
The egocentric idea that man must be in control of everything,
Constantly interfere, set us back,
Cause us to lose our focus.

We have a choice.
We have free will.
We can choose which path to follow.
If we allow it,
We will be led along a path
That leads to peace, love,
And the eternal presence of our Redeemer.
With each falling grain of sand
We are closer . . .

[November 2012]

Metaphor for Life

I have always thought of life
As a book —
Non-fiction,
An autobiography,
Each year a chapter,
With a prologue and an epilogue.

We write it as we go along,
Sometimes unconsciously,
Other times with painstaking planning and effort.
There are many characters in our book,
But we are the main one.

Every word has to do
With our thoughts,
Our beliefs,
Our actions,
Our inactions,
Our reactions,
And our perceptions of our effects on others.

As I meditate on this metaphor,
I know who writes the chapters,
But I wonder,
Who writes the prologue, the epilogue,
Those parts that precede our mortal existence
And subsequent to it?

I am not sure if the prologue
Ever gets written
Or by whom..
But the epilogue,
That part written after our mortal death,
Determined by the chapters which precede it,
That part is written by someone else.

I am not sure who writes the epilogue,
But I know it is the longest section of our book.
It has no end,
It is eternal.
I think it begins
While our newly liberated souls
Are escorted by God's Holy Angels
Into the light of His presence
And continues from there
Without end.

[November 2012]

The Male Hospital Urinal

I met this device for the first time flat on my back in the ICU
with a bladder begging for relief.

Whoever designed it must never have had to use it.

A 20-oz plastic milk-type jug with a handle, flap stopper and a
neck slightly bent upward. You use it while flat on your back.

In my case, I was wearing a BiPAP mask and a cervical collar,
could not look down to see what I was doing, plus I was wired
from ankle to chest with cables to all sorts of monitors and had
IVs in each arm.

You place it between your legs, stick in your penis and pee.
Easy, right?
Except I couldn't see what I was doing.

On my first attempt, I got the whole package in, testicles and
all, but they didn't want to come back out.

Oh, and remember—I have only one functional hand and arm,
the right. The left hand and arm now are only for show.

After several attempts, all was out, but I still had to go.

The second attempt was more successful. But then my brain
had to tell my bladder it was okay to pee in bed. The bladder
resisted that idea but finally went to work.

I don't know much about bladders. I know mine doesn't talk to me until there are more than 12 ozs. stored.

I measured volume once, filled a 16-oz. glass and had to continue in the toilet. My confidence in this jug was fading.

With the first squirt, the bottle nearly ejected off. I had to hold it in place with the handle on the topside.

As the volume and flow increased, there was a near-tsunami in the jug. Actual waves of pee heading back towards me, as this yellow flood headed toward the top of the scale.

I tried pushing down on the back end of the jug to slow down the wave action. It worked!

But when the flow stopped, I had to extricate myself without flooding my bum.

This was serious! But like a fool, I started to laugh at my predicament. I have been known to laugh at the wrong time in the past. I guess I always will.

I had to lie there for five minutes to finally get a grip on myself and remove the jug. I did—no flood.

But I learned a valuable lesson. Either turn and hang legs over the side of the bed, or call for a commode.

One more learning experience on the ALS road.

[November 2012]

To Be Healed

If I could touch His Robe
I would be healed
In mind, body and soul.
But He is not here.
He sits at the right hand
of God in heaven.

The Holy Spirit is here,
He is with me.
He has always been here,
Before my affliction.
Now as my affliction worsens,
He remains at my side.

Despite my unworthiness,
My weakness,
My foolishness,
My errors,
My sins of omission and commission,
I am never alone.
He will be with me forever,
Today, tomorrow, forever.

On that day
When I breathe my last,
When my heart stops beating,
I will realize the promise of Christ
When He said
Those who believe in me
Shall never die,
But have life eternal.

At that time
I will touch His robe
See His face,
Feel His embrace,
Healed in body, mind and soul
I will dwell in the house of God
Forever.

Amen and Amen

[Easter Sunday — March 31, 2013]

His Eyes

I am a story teller.
    I have a great imagination.
    I don't hallucinate.
    I keep track of what is happening around me,
    But sometimes I see things I cannot explain.

At church I was on my knees
    Saying prayers before mass.
    I looked around,
    Then looked up at the huge statue
    Of Christ the Redeemer
    Which adorns the wall behind the altar.

I always talk to Jesus
    Before, during and after the Eucharist.
    He floats there
    With outstretched arms
    Gently inviting everyone into His embrace.
    He welcomes you
    Regardless of who you are,
    Who you love,
    Or where you come from.
    He is our Great Shepherd;
    We are the sheep of His pasture.

But this day was different.
    As I gazed at His face,
    His eyes became alive.
    He looked directly at me.
    I had a chill, looked around to see
    If anyone else had noticed.
    When I looked back at Him
    He was still looking at me,
    His eyes aglow.

My eyes filled with tears,
    I could not see anything.
    When I was able to see again
    His eyes were fading
    Back into the gray stone of the statue.
    I saw His eyes.
    He looked at me.
    It has not happened again.

I don't know why He looked at me.
    Perhaps it was to reassure me
    That He knows me.
    Perhaps it was to confirm
    His presence in my life.
    I don't know why He looked at me,
    But I am so very thankful that He did . . .

[April 2013]

My Prayer

O Lord, My God and Savior
Creator of all that is seen and unseen,
Incline your ear to our supplications.

We, your servants, see trials and tribulations everywhere.
We pray for your guidance and grace
As we face the challenges of our lives.

We pray your strength will help
For all those who cry, hunger, hurt, grieve this day.
We pray for all those who are sick or dying today.
We pray to thank you for all you have done for us.

Lead us on your path here on earth
and bring us to your eternal presence when we die.
Amen.

[July 2013]

From Darkness Into Light

In the darkness
Something moves.
A stretch, a deep breath,
A solitary bird's opening salvo
To announce the coming of the new day.

Soon the morning's choir joins in,
Chickadees, blue jays, woodpeckers and crows.
As the light chases away the darkness
They celebrate their survival
By thanking God for the gift of a new day.
Every morning I await that first bird's chirp
To tell me I am still here.

And though I cannot sing with them,
My heart joins the choir
Rejoicing in the new day
And the glory of God's creation.

[July 2013]

Losing Things

As a human being
With all the foibles we humans have
I lose things.
I always have.

I lost my marbles.
I lost a pet.
I lost a kite.
I lost my balance.
I lost my voice.
I lost my glasses.
I lost a bet.
I lost my way.
I lost my virginity.
I lost my parents.
I lost all my aunts and uncles.
I lost my cousins.
I lost my brother.
I lost my wife.
I lost childhood friends.
I lost my heart.
I have lost things all my life.

Now I have lost my health.
Amyotrophic Lateral Sclerosis found me.
I am still losing things.

I lost my tongue.
I lost my ability to talk.
I lost my ability to swallow.
I lost strength in my neck muscles.
I lost my left arm.
I am losing my right arm.

Someday I will lose my legs.
Someday I will lose all of my voluntary muscles.
Someday I will lose my ability to breathe.
Someday I will die.

But in the meantime
I will live.
I will pray.
I will love.
I will be loved.
I will think.
I will write.
I will thank God for all the blessings I have received.
I will not give up.

[No date]

Groundhog Day

I am living the same day
Over and over and over.
The character in that movie
Was cursed to live the same day over
Until his hard heart was softened,
Until he was nice to people,
Until he found love.

My situation is a little different:
I have a soft heart,
I am nice to people,
I have found love.
Yet with minor variations
My days mirror each other.

The routine is the same.

[No date]

First Frost

There is joy in the morning.
Out of the eastern azure sky
the rising sun's horizontal rays
catch the crystals of the fall's first frost
illuminates them for an all-too brief moment
before they change back to the water drops they were before
and nourish the earth once again.

Our eyes have caught another glimpse
of the glories of nature
which happen all around us every day,
but are so easily missed as we blindly plod
through the challenges
of our days
on this blue-green orb we call Earth.

We humans get so tied up in our little worlds
we don't see,
we don't smell,
we don't hear,
we don't feel
the beauty that surrounds us every day.

It's time to slow down,
to appreciate,
to commune with the gifts
God has created.
We are here so short a time . . .

[No date]

55

The Stories

The Word "BOOK"

In my first few years of teaching, Whittier Junior High School had nearly 3,000 students in grades 7–9. Every room was used each hour of the day. Before and after school and between classes, teachers were monitoring the halls. At the end of the day, I monitored the exit doors next to my room.

Whittier was an old school, built in the 1920s, with four floors and lots of wood. Each classroom had a bookcase and storage drawers built into a wall. The doors to the building were solid oak, measuring eight feet tall, four feet wide, and three inches thick. They were like castle doors—very heavy.

One afternoon when all the students had left, I noticed the assistant principal doing something to a door. Curious, I approached to see that he was carving something into the door with a pocketknife. When I asked about his carving, he showed me how with a few cuts in the wood he could transform the word "F-CK" into the word "BOOK." I suddenly understood why I had seen the word "BOOK" carved into wooden surfaces all over the building.

They don't teach stuff like that in education classes!

The Tale of the Lion

Whittier Junior High School was an unusual four-story building. It was built into a hill. From the front, you could see two stories. From the rear, you could see all four. You entered the school on three floors: the first floor from the rear, the second floor from half way up the hill and the third floor at street level.

To provide light and air to the second floor, a section of the hill was removed, creating what looked like a moat for a medieval castle. My room had five windows that opened to the moat. We had light, air and the view of a brick wall 30 feet away—no distractions!

Several days a week I played classical music on the radio. It created a relaxed setting and introduced the students to music they had never heard before.

One morning I entered the room to find a broken window, and the radio was missing. Evidently, someone had climbed into the moat and looked in the windows for something to steal. The students were upset that *their* room had been broken into and someone had stolen *their* radio.

At this point my propensity for telling tales kicked in. Over the course of any school year, I regularly told tall tales. This time, I told my students that we would not be robbed again, that one of our second-shift janitors had a solution. His brother was a zookeeper for lions at the Detroit Zoo. He had an old lion that was about to be retired from public viewing. He arranged to bring the lion to school at night from eleven to six in the morning. The lion would be on guard in the moat all night and would be taken away in the morning. No one in their right mind would climb into a moat guarded by a lion.

60

A week later I told the students that we found one tennis shoe with lion toothmarks in it.

A week or so later, in the middle of class, the principal's voice came over the PA system, "Mr. Tremewan, would you stop by my office at the beginning of your planning period?" I said I would and went on with the lesson.

I went to his office when my planning period started. As I walked into his office, he asked me to close the door and have a seat. He looked at me with the hint of a smile and said, "Tell me about the lion . . ."

It seems that he had a call from the police department about a father and his thirteen-year-old son who were found late the previous night looking into the moat with flashlights, searching for a lion. They were not taken downtown because of the sincerity of the student's story about the lion. The principal suggested I should clarify the story with the students. I did and never used that story again.

Bertha

I met Bertha in my first year of teaching at Whittier Junior High School in 1964. She was in my homeroom, and three hours later she was in my reading class.

Although she had a sweet smile, she had a look, a glare that would melt glass. Anyone looking at her longer than she cared for would get that look, and if they persisted would get the challenge, "What you looking at?"

Bertha was an eighth-grader, about 5'8" tall, a solid 140 pounds. The onlookers who failed to glance away would suddenly find Bertha in their face, ready to punch the daylights out of them. Her short fuse caused Bertha to have many visits to the assistant principal's office for disturbing the peace or outright punching someone.

One morning during homeroom, I had a chance to sit and have a heart-to-heart with Bertha. She gave me quite an education.

At her home, there were more people than there were places to sleep. On the double bed, people slept horizontally across the bed, instead of the usual position in such a bed so that four or five people could fit and sleep there. In the living room was a large overstuffed chair with lots of padding, a very comfortable place to sit—or to sleep.

Bertha said proudly, "Every night I sleep in that chair. It is the best place in the house. Sometimes it only takes the look, but most nights I fight to sleep in that chair. I sleep there every night!" Then she smiled.

The Grifter

When the weather was good, students who ate fast or skipped lunch could go outside to chill, watch the girls (or boys) play basketball, and sometimes get in trouble.

One year we had a new eighth-grader—six feet tall, built like a gymnast, and a perfect con artist. Joe would get a basketball and shoot from different places on the court—and always miss. After a few minutes, he would choose his mark, usually a seventh-grader who had been watching him.

Joe would approach the mark, asking if he would like to share the ball and shoot some hoops. After a few minutes of sharing the ball and continuing to miss, Joe would say to the mark, "How about we play for a dollar a basket? You go first." The mark always agreed—he would shoot, make a few baskets and then miss.

That's when Joe took over. Suddenly, he became an NBA player! Shooting from all over the half court, he never missed. Within a very few minutes, the mark would be head over heels in debt. Joe, "the debt collector," would give the mark 24 hours to pay up or face a beating after school or off school property.

Time after time Joe suckered in the marks and collected until one day a mark went to an administrator for help. He had no money, no way to get money, and was scared out of his wits. Thus ended Joe's career on our basketball court.

I never saw a student who could play as well as Joe could. The sad part of this sting is that this young man, who could have been a phenomenon on any high school squad, was far too antisocial. He dropped out of school. I never heard of him again.

Doyle

D oyle was a skinny seventh-grader, perhaps five feet tall and weighing less than 80 pounds. His distinguishing characteristic was that he was bald, an unusual situation for a seventh-grader.

Years earlier when I went to school, one of my friends was balding in the eighth grade, early-onset male-pattern baldness, I guess it was. In later years he grew a beard to offset what was missing on his pate.

Doyle, however, was completely bald; not a hair on his head. If you looked closely, he didn't have eyebrows or eyelashes. According to the gym teacher, he didn't have any pubic hair either.

At the beginning of the year, while I was learning the names of all my students, I seated them alphabetically and matched faces with names. As luck would have it, Doyle ended up sitting in the first seat in the middle row, right in front of my desk.

As a teacher, I am a pacer. I move around—teaching, talking, praising, correcting and assisting all over the room.

In the first week of school, as I was walking up the middle of the room toward the front, I noticed several students focusing their attention on Doyle rather than on their lesson. When I corrected them and told them to focus on their work, I glanced at Doyle to see him digging into his scalp with the thumb and forefinger of his right hand. Somehow he had found a hair follicle, pulled it out and ate it. The reaction of the few witnesses ranged from jaw-dropping silence to gagging to nervous gasps.

Since class time was nearly over, I spoke up, collected papers with the usual banter of reminding them to have their name and date on their paper, and announcing that tomorrow when they arrived, there would be a new seating chart, and I would assist them finding their new spot as they came in.

Doyle was no longer in the front-center of the room, but in the back corner by the window. To stare at him, a student would have to turn and would see his face, rather than the back of his head. When necessary, I could easily correct that movement.

Come to find out, Doyle's behavior was not new. It had developed a few years earlier, and he was seeing a therapist for help. I was not a psychologist; I was a reading teacher. All of my students were at least three years below grade level in reading. Some could hardly read at all. My goal was to get them as close to grade level in reading as I could in their year with me.

Doyle worked pretty hard for me that year. Unnoticed in the back of the room, he would dig out some hairs, collect them in the pencil groove in his desk, and when he had collected enough, he would eat them. We came to an unstated compromise. As long as he worked hard and didn't cause any problems in class, I would not interfere with his behavior. If he lost focus or tried to get something going in class, I would simply blow away his collection of hair with a puff of air.

As I remember, I only had to do that a couple of times before he understood what the situation was. He was an excellent student for me. He made outstanding progress that year, and he always smiled at me when I approached. He taught me that I couldn't change the world, but I could realign a picture.

The Old Troll

My first classroom was five windows long with blackboards covering both the front and back walls. The blackboard at the front had an unusual characteristic—a small wooden door, about four feet tall and three feet wide, centered in the middle of the wall. It actually was an access door to facilitate maintenance of steampipes on the other side of the wall.

It didn't take long one year for a student to ask why there was a door in the middle of the blackboard. Like turning on a light switch, my penchant for story telling kicked in.

I told them that Whittier was a very lucky school. We had our very own resident troll. He used to live under a bridge, but with winter not that far away, I had talked him into staying in our school so he could remain warm. I said that the door in the blackboard was the entrance to the little room where he stayed. He slept all day and at night walked the halls like a night watchman. He was well fed because he would eat the lunches students left in their lockers. In the morning before school started, he would shower in the boys' locker room, then come back to his hideaway to go to sleep for the day.

Bob

Bob was a thin wisp of a seventh-grader, perhaps five feet tall and 90 pounds soaking wet. You never saw him without a smile on his face and a dry chuckle waiting to come out. He always reminded me of a young Bill Cosby. Like all of my students, he could not read very well.

Although I did not know it when he first entered my classroom, I soon found out he was a remarkable student of human nature. One day I was delayed returning to my room from hall duty while classes were passing. As I entered, Bob was up in front of the class doing an impression of me. He had me down pat—my walk, my gestures, my speaking patterns and my vocabulary. He was me!

He did not notice me right away when I entered, but when he did, a nervous smile flashed on his face and he moved toward his desk. I immediately stopped him and complimented him on doing me better than I did! The whole class laughed, and we all went to our lesson for the day. As Bob left, I told him he could be me anytime.

Henry

Henry was in my eighth-grade homeroom for the first fifteen minutes of every day. He was about 5'6" tall, maybe 135 pounds, but wide; not overweight, just wide. He also had one rather unpleasant characteristic—he smelled bad! The smell followed along with him as if it was an aura. Anyone within three feet would quickly become aware of him and move away.

During the first week of school, I sat down to have a long talk with Henry, just as I did with all my homeroom students. I learned that Henry lived in a small two-bedroom, one-bath apartment with his parents, a brother and his grandfather.

The parents had one bedroom, the two boys had the other, and his grandfather lived in the bathroom. The grandfather had some continence problems; he slept in the bathtub so any accidents could be rinsed down the drain. The boys had no place to go to the bathroom, wash or even brush their teeth. They relieved themselves in an area behind the garage. Henry could not remember the last time he'd had a bath.

After contacting the social worker, I developed a plan for Henry and got approval from the gym teacher and the principal. My idea was that every day as soon as Henry arrived at school, I would hand him a bag of clean underwear, toiletries and a towel, and he would head for the showers in the locker room. At that time of day, no one would be down there, so Henry could take a shower all by himself. Afterwards, he would bring me the gym bag. The next morning, I'd hand him the bag again filled with fresh, clean supplies.

Everything was set to begin on a Monday morning. Henry arrived earlier than usual with a big grin on his face. I handed him the gym bag and he headed toward the locker room.

Homeroom passed by quickly and first hour began—but no sign of Henry.

At the end of first hour, I received a note from Henry's first-hour teacher asking, "Where is Henry?" Fearing the worst, I had a teacher cover the beginning of my second hour and I headed for the gym.

When I got to the shower room, I was greeted by clouds of steam and there, standing in the middle of the main shower head, was Henry having one of the best (and longest) showers of his life.

I called to him, he came out, got dressed and headed for second hour, and I returned to my classroom. As I was leaving him, I noticed his fingertips were all wrinkled like pink raisins.

By the third day, Henry could get everything done on time and make it to first hour on time. Henry was happy, and so were all those who came in contact with him.

The Phantom

It was the beginning of another school year, just like the years of the past and the many that were to come. Every day 3,000 seventh- and eighth-graders came to our junior high school.

Before the end of September, however, we knew something was different: The Phantom Crapper had arrived.

One of our teachers returned from a planning period, opened the classroom door and found a fresh pile of excrement just inside the door. Custodians quickly cleaned up the mess and deodorized the room. While we were contemplating the editorial qualities of that mess, it happened again—different teacher, different hour. Same M.O.

The next week it happened again—different floor, different hour. We all decided to lock our doors whenever we left our rooms and to be more vigilant about who was in the hall during our planning period.

Students had to have a hall pass to leave the classroom during the day, so we even checked who was out on pass during the hour of the event and questioned them to see if they had noticed anything—to no avail.

It was a little weird. If you forgot to lock your door, you would get a present. One teacher had a special surprise. Students noticed a foul odor coming from the wooden cabinets built into the classroom wall. Investigation found the source. The Crapper had struck again.

Off and on during that school year, the phantom would strike again. By the end of the year, he (we assumed it was a male) had struck on every floor and during every hour of the day.

We never found out who he was. It only happened for one school year, so we figured he was an eighth-grader who had taken his behavior on to high school. But we never heard any more about it.

Becky

Becky was an eighth-grader in my last hour class. She was about five feet tall, with blue eyes and beautiful long brown hair. She looked more like a woman than a thirteen-year-old.

In class she was a very hard worker, laughed easily, and was having one of the best school years of her life. She was the oldest of five.

She lived about four blocks from school, so she was always there, even in bad weather. It was unusual for her to miss school, but one day she did. The next day she came in with an unexcused absence excuse and a sheepish, embarrassed look on her face. She confessed to skipping school with a couple of her girlfriends, apologized profusely, and promised never to skip school again.

The next day when she came to class, she was very upset and asked to speak to me privately. It seems an older neighborhood boy knew that she had skipped school and threatened to tell her dad unless she had sex with him. She did not want to have sex, but she said she would get a "whippin" if her father found out she had skipped.

I asked her what time her father got home from work. She said about 5:30. I told her I would come by at six and help solve her dilemma.

When I arrived, I met her father and her four siblings. I was invited to sit at the table with her father and to have a cup of coffee. I explained everything that had happened, including her sincere apology and her promise to never skip school again.

The father was wonderful. He was not happy about her skipping but felt she had been punished enough by the threat. He said he would take it from there. He thanked me for helping his daughter and invited me to come by for coffee anytime.

I don't know the rest of the story, but she didn't get a "whip-pin" and never skipped again for the rest of the year. I don't know what happened to the neighbor boy, but I suspect he learned a lesson.

The Reverend

Starting with my second year, the students in my class were those seventh-graders who were poorly prepared for junior high school. My job was to teach them basic skills so they could be successful in the eighth grade. I had five classes that year.

On the first test day, I was passing out the tests and giving instructions when I heard a commotion behind me. I turned to see one of my students on his knees praying for help on the test. After a whispered short prayer, he sat back in his desk and started the test. Most of the students looked askance at him but settled down to work.

While they were busy, I began to think carefully about the prayer and realized that the student carried his Bible with him every day. He might not have his textbook, but he always had his Bible.

After the test I collected the papers and sat on the edge of my desk. I asked the class what they thought about prayer in school. All but one indicated you are not supposed to pray in school. I told them I prayed in school every day. They looked at me like I had just grown a second head. Several students commented they had never seen me pray.

My response was, "That's my point. My prayers are between me and God." I said that I did not need to show them that I was praying. I added that there have been lots of people in history who put on a great show of praying but were not always good-hearted people. I thus stressed the point that we have the freedom to pray whenever or wherever we want to.

My soliloquy must have had an effect. The Reverend never prayed so publicly again, but he often gave me a little grin when he opened his eyes after a quick prayer.

Epilogue

So many words come to mind when I think of Paul: wonderful, kind, loving, passionate, compassionate, intelligent, strong, courageous and inspirational. So many roles he played in the lives of those around him: Flint Central High School Indian mascot, outstanding caring teacher and administrator, Civil War buff, storyteller, writer, poet, father, grandfather, friend. Paul was a valiant warrior showing unbelievable strength and courage in the face of such a terrible disease—the ALS monster.

Paul published a Civil War book entitled *As Near Hell As I Ever Expect To Be.* The book is a true story about a Civil War soldier's letters to his wife describing his experiences. The soldier had been at war for just a few months when he wrote that he was "As near Hell as I ever expect to be." Ironically, Paul found his own life with ALS to be as near hell as he ever expected to be.

Paul spent much of the last two years of his life writing inspirational poetry detailing his illness and his faith in the Lord. Lying in a hospital bed a week before he passed away, Paul felt alone and far from God. I told him to continue to depend on the Lord and pray for reassurance. As I drove home that evening, I prayed that the Lord would flood Paul with waves of love. That night Paul had a dream.

Paul's Dream

Paul and Jesus were alone on a beach by the Sea of Galilee. They talked as they walked along the shoreline. At dusk Jesus built a campfire just for Paul near the edge of the water. He cooked fish for Paul and gave him bread and wine. Finally, Jesus disappeared into the night.

This dream reassured Paul that the Lord was going to take care of him on his journey to Heaven.

Paul was a blessing from God, and it was an honor and a privilege to help take care of him. Even though he ended up not being able to walk or talk, his spirit touched so many family members, friends, students, doctors and nurses. He and I felt that God put us together for a reason. I can never be certain what that reason was, but I do know that I thank Him for putting Paul in my life.

Because of Paul I have learned:

> Do not to take life for granted.
> Our days on earth are short.
> Be a blessing to others.

Gloria Tibbetts

About Paul

A crooked smile, a scraggly beard and
thinning hair shaved clean.
A man not afraid to express himself in poetry and to share
the remainder of his life with those he gathered around him.

He was my friend.

When he could not talk, he wrote.
When he could not eat, he cooked elaborate dinners
and served us.
When he could not walk, use his arms, move his fingers or
breathe, technology extended his life in ways
we all questioned.

At the end, Paul chose to end his life as he had lived his life
with honesty and integrity.
Like the Native Americans he so admired, Hanta Yo, it is a
good day to die.

Suzanne Kristin

Additional book by Paul Tremewan, available at Amazon.com

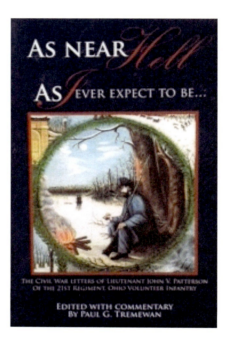

This book, published in 2011, is the true story of a Civil War soldier from Ohio, 27-year-old John V. Patterson. In September 1861, he left his young wife and two babies on their farm near Pemberville, Ohio, when he, along with thousands of other Ohioans, answered Lincoln's call to save the Union.

In November 1861, Victoria Patterson received a letter from her husband in which he stated he was "As near Hell as I ever expect to be." Over the next four years, this soldier–husband was sick, wounded, captured and imprisoned, but he escaped— and he survived the war.

Based on letters to his wife, this is an "ordinary" soldier's account of battles lost and won, of sickness, of deprivation, and always of a deep yearning to be home on his little farm with his family. Paul Tremewan fleshes out this soldier's story by giving an historical overview of some of the battles and events John Patterson was involved in.